THE GAME OF 100

Ghosts

Hyaku Monogatari Kwaidan-kai

poems

Terry Watada

We acknowledge the support of the Canada Council for the Arts for our publishing program. We also acknowledge support from the Government of Ontario through the Ontario Arts Council.

We acknowledge the financial support of the Government of Canada through the Canada Book Fund for our publishing activities.

Cover photography and design by Peggy Stockdale

Library and Archives Canada Cataloguing in Publication

Watada, Terry, author
    The game of 100 ghosts / Terry Watada.

Poems.
ISBN 978-1-927494-41-7 (pbk.)

    I. Title.

PS8595.A79G34 2014   C811'.54   C2014-902549-1

Printed and bound in Canada by Coach House Printing

TSAR Publications
P. O. Box 6996, Station A
Toronto, Ontario M5W 1X7
Canada

www.tsarbooks.com

for my brother Hideki,
Mike Shin, as good a brother as I've ever known,
and my son "Bunji", who loved both his uncles

Contents

A Game of Ghosts

night
      crept like
   smoke in a forest fire

at sundown
                  the evening
         settled and everyone sat
         in
                  a circle
around
a circle of candles.

in the brilliant
splintering   demise of
the sun,
         the timid   wax'd flames

   before the story-tellers
   flickered

and sputtered
feasting
         on air, awaiting
the smoke-filled   capsule-
bodies of
            ghosts.

tell the first story, tell
the second,
         tell the one-
   hundredth

extinguish   each
candle with each story until
the remnant of   the past
re- turns
and
        a last conversation

(precious and true)   takes place

between the mouths of the grieving and sorrowful
and
        the thoughts of the
    beloved dead   secrets are

revealed.

The Day After He Died

the morning after . . . sun-
shafts
          dappled the walls
with playful puddles
of light

i think i
          felt his
presence   the beauty
of brotherly love danced
on the walls through
window
          panes
and i laughed as he might have

he was telling
me he was fine   happy that
the pain, the thinning of
legs
          and mind, was over.

don't worry,
he said, *don't be sad just don't be*

and
     then
  i remembered mom   *okachan*

coming to me,
bedside
          the day after,

and
        she smiled as she
gently tickled   and
rubbed
          my back
in a last gesture of motherhood

no worry   no
cry   i am all   right

and all was well when the light faded
into the long evening & after-
moon   shadows

The Silent Mouths of Rain

at
    the striking of
        blue
 o' clock

when a flock of clouds
muttoned to-
gether at the denouement of

evening, i
listened
        to the mouths
   of rain
rattling   on
incomprehensibly
in a foreign   tongue

mutterings of a
child-
      hood
spent in a weeping storm

banshee barking
in
   the night
ballet-weed newspapers
flying
       flipping
  crinkling snapping
ripping down alley-
ways

the sizzle of
the steady   rainstorm
sub-
        siding into a drizzle
and sputter of
whisperings   of

long-ago dead
abuse:
        ghosts speak

but
the mouths of rain remain silent

impermanence

the pain
       of
   dark places.

1.

4-room apartment with bath and kitchen
on
      Powell Street, old Vancouver, 1937

    Mondays, mom went
    to sewing class

I stayed home
     by myself
    I was four

shadows grow into *obake*
before
     his babyeyes
   chinese breathing in

the back steam-laundry room   pipes
hiss and wizz
       with every press
for money   he shivers in the humidheat
and
    darkness

& he sits alone

in Kono's front room   only one light burns
quietly in a corner

The seed of all crime is evil; the Shadow knows . . .

a radio
a lone companion   in his murky fright

Fukushima-*san*
crashes
          into the apartment   dropping
the evilseed bottle of whiskey
and
stumbles into the bathroom

I felt a duty
& obedience rise
              to the surface
        with-in me

I grabbed the bottle,
ran to the toilet

a room of ammonia stink and withered walls

and offered the bottle
to him
        My eyes beamed innocence a smile
        of helpfulness, innocence

  He grew so angry, he growled
  loudly   like a ronin enraged
  and slapped my face

I buckled and fell
back

8

to the floor,
the whiskey spilled and stung,
my red skin
and   eyes

the light dims to unconsciousness:
The Shadow knows . . .

ll. 1939

midnight
            clatter
the imagegames   the
mind plays

Okasan tiptoed in-
to
        the kitchen
with me in tow the perfume of her
night
            gown
in my nose some comfort
as *obake* rattle in   the dark.

a flick of the light   cock-
roaches   feeding
on the butter   dish

with exposure   the *oni*bugs
scat-
        ter into dark places
    holes & wallcracks

a boy squirms   the
eyes   tingle

Okasan brushed
        off the remaining magician
insects   down
                the drain
and placed the butter dish in
the icebox
                She
        turned to me and said,

Mottanai, ne.

III. 1942

mom
        lies on a gurney
    in the hall outside the Vancouver
    waiting room of   purgatory

        (dead
    to the world
    & so they   hope)

the nuns
        ink-bottles of
compassion   with
only hate and indifference peering
out from their habits   at the enemyalien
sweating   with
        pain,
    death looms

praying for deliverance for themselves,
the sisters-of-mercy

yet he sits in the Kawai cabin in Minto
waiting
        to

    hear about *otosan* who had been
    crushed in a truckroll down
    a mountainside

he waits wrapped in
Kawai-*san's*
        fragrant (of compassion)
dark arms of concern

I heard them
talking thru the walls
late at night   conspiring to
give me away to the enemy
Japanese;
      oka dead
  otosan dead of his injuries

What else could they do?

a ten-year-old boy's eyes
tremble
        while submerging in water
as he did as a toddler,
as a child, as a teenager, as a
young
    man
as a defeated man

and gazing at an   alien
sun

IV. the 1960s

the absurdity of childhood memories
he
        forgets them to survive
to live with himself though

the house of crying women
reminds him   every
day   every where every
which way

so he runs to
blank obscurity   until
he
      bites on his lip

  holding in the pain and
  resolving to   *gaman*

in a moment of clarity, i hear my *oniisan's*
words
              of contempt, his choices . . . his failures

You have to know what you want to be so
you
      can't
  sit on the fence   forever
  choose . . . choose

You're in grade 10 for christ's sake:
doctor, lawyer, architect, engineer
you need a 90 average
            to get into
 university

Drop music,
art,
      literature,
take important subjects —
they can be hobbies to make friends

You don't have to like what you're doing
just do it   and so he betrays his own
impulses, his own   dreams

V. 1984

the hospital machines
begin
their countdown   seconds
remaining to   oblivion
for   mom and   he stands
in-
      different to the im-
plications

It's your choice
let her go I'm fine with it.

i can't make that decision. not without you.

Say goodbye & be done with it.

13

his cold heart his negation of
intimacy   brotherly love

the grief of
life &
        death
    comes over me

His   boney hand at
my shoulder   i am
a-
    lone   again

and i let mom go.

But in that moment,
he cries   breaks down,
bends over
an old porcelain sink seeking
comfort
            in the cold
    and impersonal

i rub his shoulders saying,
"it's all right . . . it's all right . . ."

knowing it   isn't

I have a brother again:
compassionate, emotional,
in his shuddering love

if only for   a time

VI. 2012

and in the days after he died
on a cool, crisp morning
i
    hear him
in
      my half-sleep

as clear as a
woman's ocean eyes deep
water-black
          & unfathomable

commanding me in his
stern voice
        Just do it.
just do it,
      so i will

in the constant shift of impermanence.

Prairie Luminescence

About twenty miles
south   of Calgary,
back
        in '46, she
walked along
a dirt road
toward   the vanishing   point

Her Eaton's catalogue
dress with a flower print
flowed
        around her
 in a sad kind of way.

the grime of
her   life
adorned her face

[trudging along in her struggle
]

She lived with
her widower father; mother
died
        of the consumption,
her body a brittle stick of
charred wood in the end

The father's younger
brother
        lived
  on the other side

in a squarish house
with his wife and two kids
but no one got along

Never
liked my brother either,
                guess
that's why
I feel sorry for her

It hurt my eyes to see her
ruby red lipstick throbbing
in   the
summer   heat

as she walked that lonely road,
dust on her white high heels.

August Light

when
    the evening
  creeps in-

to the empire of day,
the light
        turns
    nostalgic.

i can see my mother
    in her green
smock

[with clam-shells opening
and closing breathing
in desperation]

buzzing
       around
    my dad

who's sitting out-
side   beside the garden
on
a kitchen chair in
a sheet
       to keep himself
clean get-
ting
    his hair cut,
flinching at every knick
every
      itch

i   hated
her in
        that green smock
because i knew i was next:
the shaver
      and snipping
   scissors
                mosquito-
biting
my neck—the tiny
filings digging
into
      the skin
irritating to a need to scratch—

so we
sat and suffered with-
in
    the lush garden of
    Rousseau—

dark
cucumber jungle patch,
nude tomato
plants and   pear-snake   tree insects

   circle,
            looking
for an opportunity to feed.

And it is   august
i remember
most—with its warm
kind
      of light

shaded with shadows and
full
        of home,
sadness,

        and sense of loss.

By a Chinese Lamp

Laura
    Nyro
sang her siren
song
    softly
  upstairs

by a Chinese lamp
in
    my
mother's room

dragon red oriental   yellow
and tassels with
prisms
    of light
  attached

the   colours, flavour
and smells
of
    Singapore, Kowloon,
    Macau

[long-hair,
        black pools
of luxurious oil on
the shoulders—
slanted-   inscrutable
    eyes, angled
sharp as knives]

mystery
        women
in slitted *cheong sams*
intoxicating
            smoke
and evil
fingers with needles
for
    nails a 1930s *noir*
  poster in art deco style

Chinatown, my Chinatown

so soon too young
  she was gone
too   soon

the
      things   she
missed with
such a   short life

her impassioned breathing,
poetry
        on a
lover's tongue   children laughing
into
adulthood. grand- children
calling *Bachan!*
out of love and anticipation

the sauce of
conversations at dinner the loom
of darkness

weaving
the coat   of daylight

and
        the music of Laura
    Nyro

upstairs
        by a Chinese lamp
i sit on the bed
to
        contemplate
the   glow of her
absence.

and when i die . . .

Down a Country Road

sun flooded
the road   like clear
invisible
          -blue
      water

the dust between
my
      toes

  felt like i wasn't
  wearing shoes

my clothes   were loose
              my skin
full
      of light and rain
my hair   black as an ocean
sky

the dirt road up
to Ito-*san's*   barn
was
      slow-going with

dead tractors & cracked, busted
wagon beds lying in-state
on the
          grass be-side
      the processional

the wood   of sheds and

buildings
          was grey
   wormwood —
   burrowed   decayed like

broken teeth   hanging
limply from their gums

but Ito-*san's* face glowed
like
      the hinterland   an *Issei* pioneer
  surveying
  the harsh fields his fields. (finally)

the road led to a time of plenty

Mizuno-*san* wore
a
    smile like i
put on a

winter coat to keep warm
                 but
          i
            saw him

on autumn days   when
his smile
and his round full face
were   hidden
by
    bushels of tomatoes
  onions
        and cucumber

all to keep us during the winter
to come

and he laughed when i grimaced
at the *gobo* the *nasubi* the
kabocha
       he understood but
    kachan squirreled them   away
  in the cold room
              below.

his gifts led to bows of gratitude,

and the
        gravel
  road wound through
  a stand of trees

to a barking dog chained to
its house with water bowl
as weathervane

measuring rain
directing
        wind

and in the distant fields
of
    strawberries, cabbage
and lettuce uncle Harry laboured,
his
     muscled arms

       pulling
       in crop like a Colossus before
       Elysian
                plains

he loved my dad don't know why
he just did
                called him *"boshin"*
         talked in wind rushing tones
         rattling windows
         with *biru* as his Muse

he spoke English to me
only one who did as if he
were interested

he & i
         walked the fields
   one summer and he taught
   me to ride a bicycle

i wobble, i careen, i fall before
his strong hand steadies me
just
        like any uncle should

i wondered about the dog though
it
        had no name, never petted   just
        fed and
                   went unloved

a country dog driven to desperate barking
at any stranger that
came up
           the road.

a time of friendship and practical cruelty.

corn roasts in august
the humidity
             attracted
  mosquitoes as our
  guests

yet the sweet kernels
touched
          and
   then coated by
   luxurious butter

made the insects feel welcome

oka and auntie   laughed
over stories
             and
they cooked with love
and
       generosity
as ingredients

and we all watched the
sunfall
          our fire rose
higher and
             higher until it was time to go home

goodnight
        uncles, aunts cousins
laughter silenced muted talk. [i
hate the silence of missing you]

and i stepped into Ito-*san's* barn
upon reaching
                the top
      of the hill at the end of the
      visible road

the air [spangled with
dustlight
            insects of fantasy
  and pungent incense]

expanded and swelled
to fill
        the cathedral-temple
  around & above me.

i bowed before the altar of
the dead   the memories of avuncular kindness
auntie love acceptance & kindness

the sad generous facial creases
as i held out
an
      offering of warmheart   love

the only emotion I have left.
it is a time of grieving

A House of Crying Women

No One
lives in the house on Ivy Avenue any-
more   but it once was
a
    home
        of
 immigrants,

struggling to un- derstand
the language,
       the customs the
    food;

a diary of copied stories a book
of phonics a
spelling workbook

but a woman cried upstairs
for home, for country
for 3 sisters, 2 brothers for her
old-before-
her-time   mother

all dead   long before &
after
    the war
but
   she listened to
them in the   crackling
firedark hours of her life.

she heard them weeping

down the hallway shadows
    when   she
 realized she
 was all   alone

and a father
deep
       with-
  in the basement

communed   with his loving
sister
        his empty mother,
     with the ghost
     bright eyes,   and long forgotten

aunts: hearing their voices, in long ago
photographs.

and even the house next door 101
Ivy   Italians   a
community of
                Toronto immigrants
      no one felt comfortable

with the hyphen   no one was
Canadian

the italian women cried for their
lost   mother
            giving birth
    to a   dead sister

and i am nestled in the pocket
of a brother just passed

away   his wife   (despises me)
cries amongst the debris of
his life   but i sense
our mother laments   over
his soul
                perhaps forgiving
 him   for his pettiness
for his anger
and for his   stinginess

and i too am alone   in
the
        house of crying
women
thinking about him

and trying . . .
                trying
   trying . . .

to forgive.

kiyooka airs

fall-
      ing tumb-
   ling
stumbling thru
kyoto
       airs from
the balconies of kiyomizu-
dera

what is your wish?
longer   life to see . . .

to see my grand-
son
     become a
  doctor

to dance & stumble at
his
     wedding

to hear his arguments
bubble up
    and burst their logic
all over
        me

to be treated
in my grand-daughter's
clinic   to kiss
her cheek
turned red and then

pink
at her wedding

to hear her
boast
        of her successes
while feeling
my   failures.

but I   will not survive
the fall
            of   wishes
and   regrets

kyoto airs bejewelled
with light
                and stars
too jagged, too foreign, too
thin
        to hold me up

yet
        the resin trees
  breathe
            deep
as I descend   into
their depths

perhaps to come   out
into
        the light.

again

Legend has it that if a person jumps from a balcony of the Kiyo-mizu-dera temple in Kyoto and survives, his or her wish will come true.

For my brother's wish and Roy Kiyooka's dream of Kyoto
June 2012

Come With Me

Come
      with me
  warmheart   let me

feel your sea-breath hand
in mine   as it flutters and
smoothes
        my fears away

come
     with
  me

as the light disappears
at
     the sunset horizon
like all sensation
        save your
sadness
persisting as perfume on
         a hot
summer's day

come   with me
to be together   among
the black
       stars and
  celestial dreams

come with me.

I still have
my son his child-
ren   my brothers and
sister & the memory of
another   to bless, kiss   and hold

I stay
            in divine
        supplication.

no? I shall wait for you then.

Last Dream

in a courageous fight . . .
        he slipped a-
way
        peacefully in his sleep

do we dream as
            numbing death
    crawls up the   legs? do we

writhe
        in the pain of
enlightenment

or drift   into shining joy   does peace thaw
frozen   death
                    like a warm
        rain?

Or   does regret drizzle the mind

with black paint
until sunlight   crashes
into the
            western horizon of

the Buddha's gaze with no end question
on the
            lips?

a last dream:

the crying blue ocean   below   a young
blue sky
            above
balancing on a railing between   while
oka cleans the rice   of grain swish and swirl
like white pebbles
                    caught
            in a Naruta whirlpool.

a sea creature erupts the surface
a monster spirit's
guttural
            voice
belches forth and
I fall
        into the blue   below

gasping for the blue
above   drowning in
water until
a tender callous'd hand
grips my collar
                and pulls me
up
        to the indigo sun.

a last dream:

a young boy
dances   or tries to dance
to the scratchy records
on the RCA
    the rough-
hewn splintered walls of an
internment prison
rumble
   with the shuffling feet
 and sweaty hands
 on
   the backs of frayed summer
   dresses   a handprint,
      a stain
but the couples glide to the music

"My son Hideki he had first time dance to-night at Hotel.
He said to mama, 'Mama, I made dance to-night' and he was very
joyful.   We are just smile."
        MATSUJIRO WATADA, Minto, BC 1942

the walls fall a-
way   as the recordsong
crescendos
    and the forest
 trees   march to
 the musicmarchinginside to hug

the
   children in
  a leafy embrace.

the last   dream:

a cat, a grey-brown cat
mewing   goodbye
as their truck pulled away
from
        the camp

he sees it through tears
and the cat melts before his

 dreameyes

did he dream a
last
        dream? did *okasan*
in her coma? did
dad
        in the ambulance on
  his way
                to the morgue?

dark thinking eyes closed
for the last time
and
        dreams evaporated.

The Dinner

a   hollow
pocket
          hovered

around the dining-room
as dinner was served.

my
    brother
loved to play host
back in the day

he always brought out
an adequate bottle
of wine
        my father called
      him kitsui *with money*

he always stored away the bottles
any   one
         brought as a gift.
kitsui

but i should have appreciated
his little gestures   his pockets of
generosity
but too little much too late now

his wife   sat
in his son's renovated kitchen
to eat by herself in the company
of turkey carcass

        stuffing, canned cranberry
    sauce and *sushi*

in the company of her grief.

a flutter of spirit hands
in
        hushed room-
    corners
he
once asked her
to come with to where
he was going
                she
    refused of course

but i wonder
if he is calling her
towards   his
grave   *their names are together*
on his tombstone

her facial muscles
slacken   as her sadness
emerges into the
                    light

and
    her legs
  drag

as if gripped in place
by gravity or hands
grasping
            her ankles.

i wonder as she
refuses direct eye-contact
as only the perfunctory
spills
        out of
      her mouth

every time, every occasion

she blames   me
(i know) for his passing
how i
        refused
  his demands of money
  of property   of title
  kitsui   until

i held his outstretched
hand   as he poured out

      his regrets, his guilt, his
      sorrows   in rebellious tears,

      defiant
              tears
        enraged   tears
        with
              black tears
but did i forgive?

his wife pushed me aside
to comfort   to stop the
drizzle of

a crying
rainfall

i could only watch tearless
— my self lacking pity

i carried his coffin of stones
to his final resting place
a place
a fair distance from our
parents   only scorn and rejection
as his last act on this earth.

his parents   were never
my
parents

he never sat at holiday
dinner tables   unless he came
late
and then ate by himself

in the company
of turkey,
stuffing, chow
mein

perhaps i should have been the brother
reaching out for
the sake
of family

but i was not.

the holiday table is laden
with heavy
               dishes of thanks   the relatives
laugh
        with joy and remembrance
stomachs soon swell with dis-
comfort
and satisfaction

he would have been happy pontificating
on
        some obscure opera while his wife

   turned a deaf ear while others sat   with
   eyes glazed over

but that was us for a time

now we partake of plenty
while pockets of guilt, pockets of
shame
               pockets of sorrow

grow into the shadows
and corners of disappearing family.

virgin moon

in its
       first quarter

the clear (liquid) light
droplets
             of light
   bounce

and splatter the companion
gameroom

with a wish (as we all
wish):
        to talk one last time,

for a day, for an hour, a minute

to sweat
        out
   answers to hear why
   he hated me

why
he loved me

and as the revelations seep
into me
        perhaps i'd
find   it was my fault
or that nothing ever was the case.

a third of the candles extinguished
and
      the
conversation draws near.

100 Ghosts

In the corners and cross-roads of the Big Smoke

(*thank you Bunji*)

A Silent Rain

When a sliver of light
becomes a dagger of night,
the hour of cantrips
and incantations glows bright.

the Big Smoke sings
a kind
of Blues in the key of Waits:

against the steady choir
of
        traffic and sirens,
I
        slumber
in the breezy dark,
but not asleep, never asleep.

life is too short
(claims the cliché) for Poe's
slices of death to interrupt

and the rain comes beating
on the roof   in waves of
tranquility and   sadness

                against the glass
    dripping over eaves   and

soaking in-
to
        the ground
sinking in—

to
      the plateau of fantastic streets,

i   escape the self-doubt, self-
loathing,   the knife of
self:
(the fear of being found out,
the
      vanity of the hack writer)

images of melting colours, barking dogs, a loving
baby
touching my shoulder in an effort to comfort

the hour of cantrips
and incantations begins.

crying, absolute breakdown, without motherly
love

kiss   the
mouth   of phantom lovers
      (wide open
  eyes squeezed & tight)

rivulets   streaming
across
      the contours of

  cheeks, nose and
  chin

with the realization
of what is and
what

        shall be, i
    awaken
                to the rain gone
silent

I am alone in bed
with the   memory
of magic and

the streets
        continue
    to sing.

Suicide City

On a copasetic night
of cop beatings,
     street meanderings
 and wanton love-

making out
against a moist brick wall

osamu jumped
from
     the Bloor Viaduct
hitting the asphalt

not surviving even
a moment   of
clarity.

Tim Horton's at
2 a.m. dave
thinks
    about
  what he will do
  tomorrow

she's in a coma
    the stillness of a stroke
 in her brain

no chance of survival
no glimmer in the eyes
it's best

one shot to the head
and she's gone
and then dave is gone

moments later
lives become headlines

you want to die?

I am 60   a declaration
of time dwindling
                    only
20 years left anyway.

I am alone what's the
use?
        the paralysis
    of analysis
a philosophical desire
for nothingness

to sleep. to feel nothing. to
see nothing to be no-
thing
            but your dreams?

loneliness
looks for company
in
        a city of 5 million

the coldness of
skyscraper white & black

buildings the decrepit   lowrise
and tired
            Victorians

 featherlight garbage flying down
 anonymous ominous alleyways

the bodies pile high be-
hind
        the small prim hotel

    behind
    Dundas & eternity   (a portal to another
    reality)

to die of exposure is a kind of suicide
on wintry
          nights
  of cop searches and social
  worker pity

when loneliness provides a reason
to leave. to feel nothing
not even a
                dream

Lisa

As she
            lay
    die-
            ing,

her mother, as
all *Nisei* mothers
tend to do,
en-
        treat-ed
her to choose
a religion

"You've got
to have a funeral somewhere . . . "

all the relatives
will be coming all
the friends   I've got to make
arrangements:
food, flowers, the minister . . .

(like a wedding)
she had one   once;   it was
a happy day

must
        ob-
    serve
            the social
graces (
her daughter's life

was embarrass-
ment   enough)

seems like yes-
terday
        she
met and fell in
love
        with

a Black Man
a refugee from the
war for Civil Rights

    • a taboo embraced
    • a disgrace born
    • estrangement sworn

a baptist wedding:
$1000   with a potluck
dinner   yuri &
yukiko were the maids-
of-honour
with Rev (small "c" christian)
Dave
        presiding

the black &
      community
  drank,
  sang & danced

but
laughter gave way to tears

years
        of wandering
the wilderness
with a child
        born outside   with-
out blessing, with-
scorn and
            out of
    shame

came defiance   *I am not
what you say I am . . . I am soul on ice, sister
to*
    the black saints   to Malcolm,

*Eldridge, the Panthers
with the courage to create*

but then she   reached
out to her   own

   no
        one
  understood,

identified, and she spit in our
faces
and disappeared.

eventually teaching
taught
        her compassion   so
she embraced the *sansei*
ethos

—of denial, no history, the suburbs, lost customs and traditions

and wrapped a-way
her anger of her youth. to be put
away,
stored in a trunk somewhere

In her hospital bed,
her
    mother dismissed, her
child a comfort,

she struggled
against   the cancer

as Reverend [Buddhist this time]
Grant [a touch of compassion]
shared
    the *Dharma* with her

and she cried
but not out of sorrow self-
pity or the fear
of the gloom of darkness

she cried
as the enlightened   self

and closed her eyes
as the tears
solidified and glued
her
    sight   shut.

i didn't
know her well
but
     at least in
the end we
met
     in the
Buddha Dharma

and I am grateful.

Nighthawks

at
   the diner

a neon wash a-
cross
      venetian blinds
  splinters

and   lightdrop-
lets
        in-
  to the restaurant

Gerde
leaves the pieces on the floor

the flatscreens   stream
the hockey brawls for no one in particular

maybe
        Nat King Cole
     and the Tijuana brass
or Mantovani *Music to Strip By*

tired record covers
and
     publicity shots of:

 Betty Grable, Bette Davis,
 and Bogart, Bacall and even
 Johnny Mercer pinned mute
 against the wall

maybe they pay attention.
  maybe
the only ones

flapjacks   over
        easy or is that
    the eggs?

rack 'em   with an Apple Betty
for de-ssert

what's the soup today?
        split-pea, but hold
  the bacon
        any specials?

"did you hear
  the one
          'bout
  the new Jew dog?"

Gerde shakes her head and wipes the counter.

"it's a cross
        between
  a Spaniel and Bathurst

Get it?
        Do ya get it?"

Gerde half-   smiles and pours the coffee

"You know, Spadina &
  Bathurst? Jewtown?"

"Yeah, I get it. [Lot of cold
  people in Toronto.

that's why   out west
they say it's
colder
            than a heart in Toronto.]"

anti-Semitic philosophy on a vinyl spinaround
with a side of asinine

the lateness of night
turns the joint
                into
     a Brother Waits sermon while we

fall
         un-
       to our beers

and we turn to the blues in a
Hopper
           painting
sipping cups of   coffee   while

dreaming
            about
our tomorrows
and
knowing *there ain't none.*

while i listen
to some   asshole
coming

on
to old Gerde whose
broken teeth
speak of   romance decades ago

he
just wants some company   [she
                just
        wants   to go home

and i want to listen
                to the
next record

nighthawks at the diner

while
        i
    eat
            my blue-plate   special:

sweet & sour   porkchops

    with a side of fries, slaw
    and topped with

melancholy.

The Heart

of
      Saturday night.

Richard's   a once fabled resto
at the inter-section of
Dundas and   a
tea room: hooker- infested
and
      long dead,

Tom waits on the
phoney-
          graph
singing
his   gravelled
blues
      for the days that
have gone by-bye

i sat with Judy   long ago
her
      future cloaked in

  a confusion of
  unrequited   love affairs

a gurgling child
with fetal alcohol syndrome
its
      face

  distorted its mind

conflicted confused edged
with death

her soul
seared with hate and the love
of the father,

but not that night;
no,
an evening of scampi and
wine

the grapefruit wedge after the appetizer
don't   ask
for more   bread

you may be thrown out like garbage
into
        Dundas

    rainywet asphalt smeared with
    deadbodies in the alleyway

died of broken hearts & exposure

hookers and homeless circle;
a concrete street
with
the filmore beckoning

with mascara'd
women
            in nylon-meshed
    legs

Richard, the brawny scot
proud of his food   once
threw out a sold-out
night of
            CBC
   cognoscenti   idiots of

fashion   because they
demanded   butter
for their bread.

Judy's eyes   cobalt glo of
eyes candle-sparkled
blue   bright
     spiked

a hint of evening   as if
telling me
             maybe we
     will
           be
one.

[a hint of the working class in her sharp
cheeks, in her eastend voice]   short height &
hunger

but no, no
such
      thoughts in our
   search for the heart of most nights,

her lips soft   her rose perfume
reminiscent

of a rainstorm   her hair   as
luxurious as an
erupting coke bottle

I don't deserve her,
my
        arrogance
   exceeds my asian desire
   and vanity of my worthless-ness

we drove the streets towards
the east-
end   deadend hopes
as the   wheels   sizzled
in
        the rain that night.

i never
     saw her again
deadlost in the ever-changing
swirl
          of events
but i wander back to that night
every time
i stand outside the window
of that emptydead restaurant
of long-ago meals
                  and
     afterhour drinks in the
     denouement of

    a   cityscape
          evening.

those were the days of roses, of poetry & prose and

his voice
was
        weak, the last time
I spoke to him

on the telephone, a landline,
A tribute to
our
        youth
        misspent & wasted
[ ]

there was a rasp
to it
        like a voice from the grave.

he
    was saying
goodbye.

from a nursing home up Christie
in-to the
Avenue Rd after-
hours
        club playing Evans
heavens bill evans
on a beat-up up-right   getting
those syncopations
and
modulations right   a *Waltz for Holly*
he
        was caught by her shadowed smile

siren lips

her ardent bosom   and   twisted
tangled legs
                        they ended the night near
Chinatown
                a lower Bathurst
apartment. of peeling wallpaper, musty smells of
meals half attempted, half eaten.

an artist's loft; an intellectual's conversation coffee-klatch
right
        down
to deco posters, Sylvia Plath and cheap brandy   with
marijuana images on the side

a decades long love-affair the
poetry
        of angst and
    the music of   suffering

ended   with amputated legs
(shapely legs)
in   her sanctification in a
hospital bed   far from that

cigarette-caked smoke
burdened
            genius-filled-
    conversations
    jazz-club   with the scratchy
    Dizzy Gillespie   mingus
    parker records

revolving as sonorous horns swirled
into

the romantic unholy night.

goodbye roy

    "i'll talk to you soon," he said with faint hope

l could
       feel him
  sigh, bent over and perhaps
  fallen
      into
          his regrets

as l held my own middle of despair
bemoaning
       the
    loss of jazz, artists and red-lit

nightclubs i never knew.

Closin' Time at the 5 & Dime

the neon buzzes
           underneath the
Coffeetime Donuts sign

in the attempt to be cheerful,
    welcoming
                    but
Gladys
is
working the last hour of a 15-hour shift

the light coats any goodwill
with apathy
                    with a kind of sepulchral mask

and she is limping
on withered legs   ulcerated and dripping pus
just
      to get the order right

a crueller, honey-glazed,
cake donut with a double-double

medium size coffee, forget the Venti/
grande, tall-short shit?

a snap of the bag and a pour out of the carafe
and that's all she wrote.

"this here place
used to be a Dairy Queen"
                    that's right.

my dad used
         to bring me
    for a butterscotch dip cone   on

a hot summer's day the edible oil product dripping
onto my arm
                 we bought
our christmas trees here i always got the back end
carrying it home. That's my dad—strong, honest

i   loved his immigrant eyes

once,   i worked all afternoon
washing my
brother's car, a pugeot, and
he flipped me a quarter   to buy
a small soft cream cone here;
as
he drove away   I realized he never helped. We
never
         did anything together.

the light
          clears
    the facial shadows
and she appears bloodless   maybe think-

ing of bill, her husband lying
dead
of cancer   during the ice storm of '69.

"the manager can't make it in so
   I do a double shift. [a double-double

in a small cup of hands]
                              but
    I get   all next week off."

"With pay?" don't know actually.

Gladys begins
        singing a song
from somewhere deep in her past

rasping like sandpaper   she
can't carry a tune in a bucket   as i
do a twist and turnout
                        into
      the darkly streetlit night.

closin' time

The Game Nears Its End

characters
          in a waits scenario
like Subarus in a dogbreath
street
          limp, slump and slouch
towards a Bethel-night of

night clubs
              dives
    and jam sessions
closed-down in concupiscent
curds   of flaccid afterglow

the extinguished smoke
from
       candles (almost
   to 100)

rise up into the faint light
like
      ghosts
  suspended in the still coughing
  air

it's nearing the time
just
a few more stories a touch
more   ghosts
and expect a visitation
in
total darkness and cloying fumes.

the flicker of the past
will enlighten

100 Ghosts

The Michael Poems

For Mike Shin

Vanishing Point

Mike, his name   is
Mike.   Not Michael
though
          his mother, girl-
  friend then   wife

gave him that name
as an affectation, out of
affection.

i know you're
out
        there
  riding the highways

while the blue-meanie wheels chase
you
want you   hate you

but I knew him as Mike.
and
          Mike it will always be

get thru 'em, baby,
                get thru
      'em
he
      was
a working man

worked his father's
warehouse   at least, his father

was the manager

Mike did every-
thing:
          took
deliveries, did inventory
got coffee   moved racks
around   swept up

mostly he drove the Econoline van

a Dodge Challenger belched
and revved at
a standstill   flat on the screen
deep
        in
            the darkness
of   the theatre

the car squealed and
peeled
          out like
   a soul out of hell seeking

the
     good grace
of God

"gotta get moving"

cigarette
          hanging
   perilously from the lower lip keeping
   the cancer away

leather jacket and shades
even
in sub-zero weather

he was cool   like
Kowalski
          leaning on
   his 1970 Challenger

Colorado plates   OA5599

   looking at
   the end of days   sneering and not caring.

the ethos of the highway;   the philosophy
of the   open   road

we rode the freedom freeways of
California

          the last American hero
          the last beautiful free soul
          on this planet

a blind
          dj
   finding self-acceptance

in being black
on
      the airways

reaching out on
      the currents of the

Santa Ana
          winds to

find the ghost Kowalski

and
      the kindness of counter-
      cultural strangers

an old jagged prospector   a
bangled
          beaded
    hippie   a
free, naked spirit of love
on a motorcycle

Delaney & Bonnie & friends
Rita
      Coolidge Cherokee
  Nation refugee

 singing like a Jesus-freak

we followed
a Stingray   at 100+ mph
          on Highway 101
Mike
spotted a red light on his dash

[Fuzz-buster to avoid
        radar-traps
  by the   highway patrol]

the light extinguished
and Mike pulled over

a cruiser
swooped down
from
    its
  mountain perch
  and nabbed the Vet

jailtime in a speed-trap town

Mike and his sixth
driving   sense.

Cisco CA Ruth's
66 Café
      Ethel's
  Café two countertop dives

more
than the town needs

rusted car carcasses
beneath the
Chevron Supreme   Mobil \Gas
and
      shell signs

he smiled and ran
head-
      -long
into those bulldozers.

he knew, he knew   he
had reached the point.

California sun reflected
on his
        tinted glasses
  but never   penetrated

he'll always be Mike

we gotta get moving   we gotta
get moving on
on
      towards

our own cinematic vanishing point.

Playing Pool

On a hot Saturday night
in the air
          -conditioned reek
of sweat, day-old alcohol
& mental work-a-day
stress

playing
          pool
  with Mike   the AC pings,

clangs and chirps
like a Chinatown shopper
looking
      for a bargain on
  west Dundas

at the intersection of immigrant &
Huron

with the Lee Family Association above and
Ka Hee noodle house at ground level,
the ol' time Spadina
Pool Hall moulders in the basement

but Mike
and me swim through the humidity &
around speedbump tables with
warped cues
      studying the
  position of

reds and colour'd. Lookin' to score a run or two.

[Break]

the Shooter looks
to sell fake Rolexes in the washroom
dark in there with rust rings around the
thrones
            at the bottom of urinals the ammonia
  smell covers, cleans & seals the deal
(there's no works inside—don't buy it)

[cherry in the corner—set up for the black,
settle for the pink in the side]

Sally
holds a cue like a man's penis delicate-like

sits on a stool
like
    it's her latest castoff boyfriend
  shows off her legs   in nylons enmeshed

her sunken cheeks   crepe-rippled skin
and
      eroded eyes
  makes a man think   but
  he has a go
  what else's he got to do

with a half tank of gas and a paycheque
barely cashed in his pocket?

[sold out the 2-ball combo, pot the blue ball
  as a prize]

a fight breaks out between   the owner Doug
and
a regular, too drunk to fight effectively;
a swing of a 20-weight cue
catches a corner
of a head—crack—down he goes
rolling under
a table, blood leaving a slime trail behind.

the drunk recovers eventually stands
and stumbles to the stairs

"I'll get you, you cocksucker . . . I'm
  coming back with a gun . . . "

[run the colours: yellow, green, brown blue, pink, black
  hooked & scratch]   Mike
  wins

Mike & I
talk about girlfriends
his folks his job the community
we laugh   he
spills
        his opinions on
    the table and I listen pick

up the
pieces of the conversation
and give in
to the idea that marriage
ain't
        for him that
Springsteen is the greatest
that
        moving out isn't a good idea

"Who's a better cook than my mom?"

and I listen; and i agree;
that's my part in all this
and I don't mind
because
          we're good buds

and will stand together until the end—
it's tragedy that goes on living

~

and the evening does end as
every Saturday does
          steaming our faces
    above a bowl of

wonton mein
while the beef & greens on rice is
prepared in the open immigrant kitchen

"Man, we could eat in those days."

me and Mike chew over
life
          as life flows in & around
          us

on wild Saturday nights
in

the darkest
parts of a fragrant Harbour of dangerous
China-

      town.

Babies in the River

turning upriver   from
        where the DVP
    drains
            into
the lake,

            where
    Jilly's bumps and grinds

to Hall & Oates   in the grimy
din
        and dim lights of

alcohol   and treason

driving up-river
with Mike's
ghost   looking for   a Mac's Milk for
June's
        breath-mint

    the suburban-girl's shield
    against
            embarrassment.

Pretty Flamingo
on
        the radio

    La-la-la la-la-la pretty flamingo

reminds me of a time when

bop turned to pop
to make   money.

Who could blame 'em?

teeny boppers sweating to the beat
as opposed to
                    cigarette-filled clubs
        with needles
                        going into
 arms   and betrayal on the lips
 of
        women with cracked teeth
            and alcohol eyes
        swimming in dreams

in
        the asphalt current
that
            sweeps   into

Chinatown   duck, chicken and pig
carcasses   hanging
on hooks with expressions of
surprise,
                agony and still death
        on their faces   but

their skins are crisp, their meat succulent
as cooks

        take 'em down
        to slice and coat with
        jewelled oil and spice

Mike lights   up
a favoured cigarette
from
        his flip-top
box of Player's   the smoke
co-mingling

   with his ectoplasmic
   film
           making him visible
   to the mind's eye.

"Soba?" he suggests.

and there we were sittin' in the *Congee Star*
in
      a suburban strip-mall outpost

 - his voice edging softer
   towards silence with every puff
   and slurp

   and me wondering]
   how long's he got? can't believe
   he's dying   won't believe.

That cigarette dangles
              from his lips as
      the raw news streams   into the car

By the Jersey shore:
2 men
        and 3 teenaged boys
   were charged with gang-raping a

7-year-old girl   who was sold by her
15-year-old
             step-sister during a party
in Trenton, New Jersey   the Rowan
Towers
             the step-sister went to a party
             and the little girl tagged along
             because she was worried about her
             sister's safety

the sister had sex for money
and then took money to let the
men
             touch the little girl

touching turned to forcible sex

boys conspiring
crime on
the 506 Carleton Car screeching past
the
        Don
swearing with their ignorance
and wearing their 59-Fifty caps
sideways
to demonstrate their stupidity

    indifferent passengers
    gazing at the grocery store
    killing fields where an immigrant
    was gunned down for who-knows-what.

where masked men broke into
a midnight
meal at the *Jun Jun* and

opened
        fire
    like the *Law & Order* theme

just for kicks.

But quietly flows the Don
as Dr. Sun Yat Sen

    waves optimistically to
    the passers-by   hopeful
    of tomorrow's sunshine

which
spreads out and down into the park   a-
cross to the cityscape   into
the dissent and dissipated

        into
                        St James Town
            into

Regent Park   into Rosedale into the
Jarvis Street blues

by a riverbank, labelled
"Medical Waste"—yellow plastic
bags
        like so much garbage tossed
mindlessly
into
        water.

Naked babies
            below
     the Guangfu River bridge

and the Shandong Broadcasting
Co.
        expressed con-
cern   over the area's drinking water

lapping, restless
waves - rocking the babies
to
      sleep

without comfort or dreams

the Don River takes
a wicked right crashing onto   the beaches of
East York's
                        landscape
and Mike's ghost opens his mouth like
he has something
to say

but
he totalled the car
as he backed down
the street while

his nerve endings frayed
and his brain
bled   memories

like   the mouths of
babies   open

94

just beneath the surface   like
                tea cups
filled with the
muddy water of indifference
and
        cruelty
of a people trying to save money

turquoise identity
bands
            the only blue of
    the water.

and the chinese government
calls it an "environmental problem"

away from the river
and in-
            to
the sterility of the roads
criss-
        crossing and
    inter- secting

on the red.

The East York bungalow
low-risers   trying
for respectability hiding
secrets
from the river   where no
one can hear the crying-screams
of
a seven-year-old

from
        the rotting
mouths of babies
in
        the river.

All the worldsadness on the radio as Mike &
me listen
in the '69 Chevy machine.

A Period of Glowing Life and [Happy]-ness

the longer   l
live   the more life
takes
            away.

i remain its chronicler

~

the kitchen   that's the best
memory—

  a breakfast nook
  where we all sat a-
  round.
            a dull light overhead
Mike, Carol, Michelle,
Phil,
        Bobby.
names laughing with human frailty,
of dreaming at what was hoped to be

Mrs Shin   tall, lanky and beautiful
in her love of life
                buzzing
      around, making sure

we were
        all fed

Stephen flying in and out as if
dancing

—his profession in years
   to come

and the men Miki
and Mr Shin   wise and Buddha-like
   on the couch
enjoying
            the Pro Am
      or Masters   or
British   Open

I   take it all in:
         the gossip,
   the advice,
               the opinion

and cigarette smoke
always cigarette smoke.

I reveled in
the sense of family

in
     the noise of family
in the [Happy]-ness of
fam-
         ily

and then June
joined . . .

a highschool loyalty born to
her   beauty
        a charm
  in her love
            of Mike

and razor wit   in
her outlook on life so young
to be so   cynical   yet
conventional in
suburban ex-
        pectations
in degree of involvement

they all had that: college education, job, marriage, kids
two weeks' vacation a year   promotion prosperity
in a ranch-style/split level house barbecues, swimming pool,
luxury cars (2 of course)   four weeks' vacation   retirement   bliss
with grandchildren

but working class neighbourhoods
left
    in
  our past   and present   were filled

with love as companion   with blood
con-nect-ions
as
    joy

and all their moves   to
the near boroughs
[a white-walled split-
back-flat-house

        with garage and driveway
        luxury

but the ever-present
breakfast
        nook   still
held us in a half-circle of
family   of the stories,
laughter and back-slaps
we had
        come to expect to
    en-joy

and then the migration
the move to the distant suburbs out-
side the city

barbecue'd and mortgaged
that's all my life's been

the allure of
prosperity the trappings of
wealth   a labyrinth house   with
     unfinished basement,
[a future project]

3-car garage   friends nearby
the nearness of
      relatives as help
  and comfort

daycare centres
handle me with care   night school

and Mike fell into himself
gripped by silence   day by
day
       parents evaporated into nothing

city friends
                  abandoned for the FTD
[not the florist but fronto-temporal-dementia—
a silent disease i nor anyone had heard of—
a
     killer by stealth in the night]
sister, brother-in-law, nephews, nieces
embroiled
in   disorienting and
  crushing legal torts and threats

in Chancery

yet the circle of conversation
continues
                  in the half hug of the
  breakfast nook.

there was a
period of   glowing
              life and [
     happy-ness] now broken
by absence and the tragedy
of disease
              of misunderstanding
  of accusations and recriminations

  of poetry and love songs
  old songs I once heard

I am not a relative
        barely a friend
but
there was a time . . .

while listening to Van Morrison

the
        wind   rivered
   across
                and
through the whiteroom

like his voice   was spilling out
of
        the stereo console.

he seemed   angry
     secretive,
                    mystic
and eternally   Celtic.

the music a strange
under-
pinning for Mike lying

     in bed
                his eyes clouding
blind
like water as it freezes

yet his
fixed stare remains
                    without
      thought
                as time
drips to a slow meaning-
lessness

memories of children,
wife,
      relatives and
friends   gone

but his father lingers

his image of
     emaciated arms   kindling thin
  only good for
          burning/cremation
fell like
       ashes

the image of
the last
      long
  cigarette
dangling from the mouth

he unable to take it to
flick the ashes   unable
      to take it
out of the mouth
to say   goodbye.

but Van sang
coolly of
      astral weeks
   careening

through the spiritual
skies
      and finding
   stars of eternalnothingness

Mike's mind turns crystal
unable to form   concepts   unable
to hear the echoes of
a slipstream
                unable to
drive   along
the California coast   as
we once did
                so long ago

tears well in my eyes
but
      they don't run
as all his dreams
come
        tumbling
   down

as was his beautiful vision.

The Vanishing Point

call him James Dean, Brando,
Cool Hand   Luke   Bullitt;
just don't call him Michael.

we're driving towards coolsville
with Waits groaning with a
hang
        over
on the Blaupunkt

i see the blonde smile
in
     the shrine of the
  sun

rain   fell
like liquid sun-light

she came from Coolsville
a
     mythic town of ancient
dreams   but i saw her
her burnished legs
shown
        off
  by a miniskirt

and i fade away as Mike
goes on
his one-arm around June,
his best girl as she smokes listening
to Whitney   on the radio

105

his other arm
on the steering wheel of
his dad's Oldsmobile

but then even she evaporates
as the white lines
converge &
point
towards a lonesome expresslane

and Kowalski smiles
as
super soul
on KOW 980 screams

out the eulogy:

the last American hero
the golden driver of the golden west
ripped apart   the last beautiful free
soul on this planet.

Coolsville is just round the bend
and up the road a bit

~

the one hundredth
story told   the one hundredth
candle
            snuffed

darkness falls with a thud
can't
        you see?
    can
  you not see?

a ghostly   visitation

A Visitation

Take the last lit candle
in hand
          & realize
everything is burning

ask yourself—What is burning?
Desire

gaze at the flame
          (enter the self,
blow
        out the light
and sink into the darkness of
Nirvana

a presence gathers   the cling
of
        rosewood & ashes

he appears with piteous
raiment   of the past:
silent
        remote
    reproachful

"what is it like?
  death, I mean."

my first sensations in the great divide beyond
were open to the summit possibilities of atmic
visions

watery   like
looking in a glass
darkly   in a Lewis Carroll
fantasy entertainment

i like
          being
    dead   Of the world

there's no cold   there's
no   hate
          there's no pain.

only peace

in life i committed the three sins
greed: *i tried*
          to steal from you   because
i was the first son

anger: *i resented the fact of you*
my
          parents insulted me   dismissed me
      belittled me   allowed you to be very lucky

ignorance:
i
      thought i did not love my parents
i did not love you.

Stupid became my name.

i wish i
would've been generous, compassionate   and wise
i had so much   family, home   & love so much to give

scenes from a deathbed:

as my father said to me
when *okasan* died:

"we only have each other now"

Oniisan
            burst into
      tears as he reached for my hand

to say goodbye.
I had a brother once more
(at least, for a time)

don't cry   te-bozu
my
            love is still with you that is
      what
                  remains of me

Of
      the world

listen to the words of our past
& realize the gift you have been given:

[Death has no meaning;
when I think of the moment
of my death,

I grow sad at the loss of
warm family memories.]

our *ojiichan*
Iwakichi Takehara feb 1944

[Last night I dreamed
I was running, dragging the wind
along with strong arms]

our *otochan*
Matsujiro Watada march 1984

[My life cycle
gradually   fades to
the same unknown
               faced by our
        Ancestors

may it be as interesting as the journey
along the karmic wheel]

your *oniisan*
Hideki Watada 2004

                          ~

the candles
        are put out
    not   even smoke remains

moon-
         set at
    night

       as it sets
for every- one

the rise
      of a virgin moon
head to the north, face to the
west

     Nirvana

Glossary

Bachan	grandmother
Biru	beer
Boshin	boss
Cheong Sam	Chinese short dress
Gaman	persevere
Gobo	burdock root
Issei	first generation Japanese Canadian
Kabocha	Japanese squash
Kitsui	tight (cheap)
Mottanai ne	phrase: What a waste.
Naruta	region of Japan where whirlpools are plentiful
Nasubi	eggplant
Nisei	second generation Japanese Canadian
Obake	ghost, monster
Ojiichan	grandfather
Okachan, okasan, oka	mother
Oniisan	oldest brother
Otochan, otosan	father
Oni	devil
Ronin	masterless samurai
Sansei	third generation Japanese Canadian

Terry Watada is a Toronto poet, novelist, playwright and essayist, and historian, musician and composer, with numerous publications to his credit. Five of his plays have received mainstage production. He contributes a monthly column to *The Bulletin*, a national Japanese Canadian community paper. For his writing, music and community volunteerism, he was recently awarded the Queen Elizabeth II Diamond Jubilee Medal. His published works include *The Sword, the Medal and the Rosary* (manga, 2013); *Kuroshio: The Blood of Foxes* (novel, 2007), *Obon: the Festival of the Dead* (poetry, 2006); *Ten Thousand Views of Rain* (poetry, 2001); *A Thousand Homes* (poetry, 1995); and *The TBC: the Toronto Buddhist Church, 1995 – 2010* (2010).